첫 번째 그림 사전

동물
First Picture Dictionary
Animals

돼지
Pig

토끼
Rabbit

나비
Butterfly

여우
Fox

일러스트: 안나 이바니르

www.kidkiddos.com
Copyright ©2025 by KidKiddos Books Ltd.
support@kidkiddos.com

All rights reserved. No part of this book may be reproduced in any form or by any electronic or mechanical means, including information storage and retrieval systems, without written permission from the publisher, except in the case of a reviewer, who may quote brief passages embodied in critical articles or in a review.
First edition, 2025

Library and Archives Canada Cataloguing in Publication
First Picture Dictionary - Animals (Korean English Bilingual edition)
ISBN: 978-1-83416-600-1 paperback
ISBN: 978-1-83416-601-8 hardcover
ISBN: 978-1-83416-599-8 eBook

야생 동물
Wild Animals

호랑이
Tiger

사자
Lion

기린
Giraffe

코끼리
Elephant

원숭이
Monkey

✦ 기린은 육지에서 가장 키가 큰 동물이에요.
✦ *A giraffe is the tallest animal on land.*

야생 동물
Wild Animals

하마
Hippopotamus

판다
Panda

여우
Fox

사슴
Deer

코뿔소
Rhino

무스
Moose

늑대
Wolf

✦무스는 수영을 잘하고 물속에 잠수해 식물을 먹을 수 있어요!
✦A moose is a great swimmer and can dive underwater to eat plants!

다람쥐
Squirrel

코알라
Koala

✦다람쥐는 겨울을 위해 견과류를 숨기지만, 가끔 어디에 뒀는지 잊어버려요!
✦A squirrel hides nuts for winter, but sometimes forgets where it put them!

고릴라
Gorilla

반려동물
Pets

카나리아
Canary

✦개구리는 폐뿐만 아니라 피부로도 숨을 쉴 수 있어요!
✦A frog can breathe through its skin as well as its lungs!

기니피그
Guinea Pig

개구리
Frog

햄스터
Hamster

금붕어
Goldfish

개
Dog

✦어떤 앵무새는 말을 따라 하고 사람처럼 웃기도 해요!
✦*Some parrots can copy words and even laugh like a human!*

고양이
Cat

앵무새
Parrot

농장 동물
Animals at the Farm

소
Cow

닭
Chicken

오리
Duck

양
Sheep

말
Horse

작은 동물
Small Animals

카멜레온
Chameleon

거미
Spider

✦타조는 가장 큰 새지만, 날 수는 없어요!
✦*An ostrich is the biggest bird, but it cannot fly!*

벌
Bee

✦달팽이는 등에 집을 이고, 아주 천천히 움직여요.
✦*A snail carries its home on its back and moves very slowly.*

달팽이
Snail

생쥐
Mouse

조용한 동물
Quiet Animals

무당벌레
Ladybug

거북이
Turtle

✦거북이는 육지와 물속 모두에서 살 수 있어요.
✦A turtle can live both on land and in water.

물고기
Fish

도마뱀
Lizard

부엉이
Owl

박쥐
Bat

✦부엉이는 밤에 사냥하며 청각으로 먹이를 찾아요!
✦An owl hunts at night and uses its hearing to find food!

✦반딧불이는 밤에 빛을 내어 다른 반딧불이를 찾아요.
✦A firefly glows at night to find other fireflies.

너구리
Raccoon

타란튤라
Tarantula

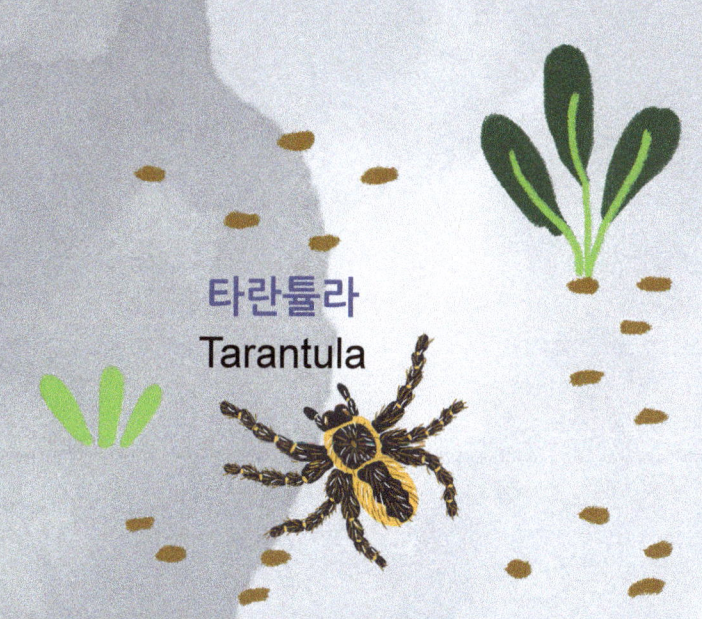

다채로운 동물
Colorful Animals

플라밍고는 분홍색이에요
A flamingo is pink

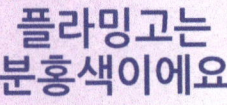

부엉이는 갈색이에요
An owl is brown

백조는 하얀색이에요
A swan is white

문어는 보라색이에요
An octopus is purple

개구리는 초록색이에요
A frog is green

✦ 개구리는 초록색이기 때문에 잎 사이에 숨을 수 있어요.
✦ *A frog is green, so it can hide among the leaves.*

북극곰은 하얀색이에요
A polar bear is white

여우는 주황색이에요
A fox is orange

코알라는 회색이에요
A koala is grey

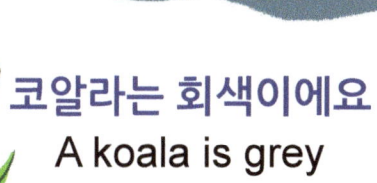

흑표범은 검은색이에요
A panther is black

병아리는 노란색이에요
A chick is yellow

동물과 새끼들
Animals and Their Babies

소와 송아지
Cow and Calf

고양이와 새끼 고양이
Cat and Kitten

✦병아리는 알에서 태어나기 전에도 엄마와 대화해요.
✦A chick talks to its mother even before it hatches.

닭과 병아리
Chicken and Chick

개와 강아지
Dog and Puppy

나비와 애벌레
Butterfly and Caterpillar

양과 새끼양
Sheep and Lamb

말과 망아지
Horse and Foal

돼지와 새끼 돼지
Pig and Piglet

염소와 새끼 염소
Goat and Kid

www.ingramcontent.com/pod-product-compliance
Lightning Source LLC
LaVergne TN
LVHW072101060526
838200LV00061B/4788